MW01716889

A counting book
presented to

with love,
from

Dedicated

to
dad

for inspiring us to love numbers
when we were wee kids

and to

Nigel and Mattie

may you and every kid out there
find the fun in numbers too!

ISBN 978-0-9844378-4-9
Library of Congress Control Number 2011921985
Copyright © 2011 by Kite Tails LLC
All rights reserved

Yum and Yuk

Duck, Duck, Duck

by

Nannette Nocon

Yum wishes!
Nannette Nocon

Arabic
Bengali
English
French
German
Hindi
Italian
Mandarin
Portuguese
Russian
Spanish
Tagalog

STARRING

and

illustrations by

John Kastner

WAHID
ek
one
un
eins
EK
uno
yi
um
odin
uno
isa

1

ITHNAN
du-i
two
deux
zwei
DO
due
ÈR
dois
dva
dos
dalawa

2

THALATHA
tin
three
trois
drei
TEEN
tra
SAN
tres
tri
tres
tatlo

3

ARBA'A
char
four
quatre
vier
CHAAARA
quattro
si
quatro
chetyre
quatro
apat

4

KHAMSA
pa(n)ch
five
cinq
fünf
PAANNCH
cinque
wu
cinco
pyat
cinco
lima

5

SITTA
chhoi
six
six
sechs
CHHAH
sai
LiU
seis
shest
seis
anim

6

SAB'A
siete
seven
sept
sieben
SAAT
sette
oi
sete
sem
siete
pito

7

THAMANIYA
saat
eight
huit
acht
AATH
otto
BA
oito
vosem
ocho
walo

TIS'A
aat
nine
nuef
neun
NAO
nove
viu
nove
deyvat
nueve
siyam

9

'ASHRA
dosh
ten
dix
zehn
DAS
dieci
SHI
dez
desyat
díez
sampo

10

AHADA 'ASHAR
egaro
eleven
onze
elf
GYRAARAH
undici
SHIYI
onze
odinnadstat
once
labing isa

11

ITHANA 'ASHAR
baro
twelve
doce
zwölf
BAARAH
dodici
SHI'ÈR
doze
dvendadstat
doce
labing dalawa

12

"Not everything that can be counted counts,
and not everything that counts can be counted."

- attributed to Dr. Albert Einstein

1

For every book sold, another will be given to a child who could use a little hand in life.

One for one, a Yum choice.

The original paintings for this book were executed in gouache.

For All Ages

www.whatsupwithyuk.com

Printed in
Rochester, NY
USA